HOW TO SURVIVE A GOVERNMENT SHUTDOWN

50 WAYS TO SURVIVE ANY GOVERNMENT SHUTDOWN OR ECONOMIC CRISIS

BY EVERETT MOSS

©2019

Download my other book titled "Survival Foods"! Go to

In this book, I'll share with you exactly what foods you should be stock piling to prepare for an economic crisis!

TABLE OF CONTENTS

Intro

Let's face it, we are living in scary times, were Governments shut down, Presidents and political parties fight amongst each other which in turn ultimately impacts the citizens.
While those in power play bad politics the people are left to figure out how they will survive. In a Government Shutdown, or Economic Crisis, thousands of people can be negativity effected and the economy can be harmed. I created this book to help you not to be a victim of these conditions. If you follow the principles and tips in this book it will help you, your family, and your friends to survive any Government Shutdown, Recession, and Depression.
Let's dive right into the 50 most important things that you can do to survive a Government Shutdown, Hard Times, or an Economic Crisis.

Chapter 1: Mentality

This first chapter we will focus mental state that you will need to have in order to survive a Government Shutdown. Having the right mindset is the first step to surviving an economic crisis.

Number 1
Plan for the worst and hope for the best.

A cliché, I know. But that is the truth. Questions such as how you will cope and how will you live will pass your thought as you stay up nights thinking what you could or should have done to mitigate the scenario in the first place.
Acknowledge now that there will be concern and panic and realize this is WHY you prep. Prepping is the insurance policy that will help see you via hard times.

Number 2
Acknowledge that there will be fear and panic.
Those of you that have gone through a disaster, poor health, job loss, or civil disobedience and combat will recognize that concern and panic are inevitable. Realize that in the case of any financial disaster, there is not a darn thing you can do other than get better and survive!
☐
Number 3

Maintain your faith.

If you are a spiritual person, discover comfort in your faith. And if not, gather your inner power and have trust in yourself and in the miracle of your life. Hold this faith close to your heart, and when difficult times come, it may be all that you have left.

Number 4
Behave productively and control upsetting thoughts.

Allowing honest truth helps manage your thoughts and change your emotional states, which are actually essential to effective habits. The options you create when you are actually faced with problems determine how rapidly you'll find a solution.

Also, when you're confronted along with a trouble you can certainly not fix, like the loss of an adored one, you make choices regarding just how to react.

Useless actions, like fussing or even tossing an empathy party, will certainly keep you stuck Those actions will definitely rob you of your mental stamina.

Control upsetting ideas. Your thoughts may be your enjoyable possession or your biggest adversary. If accept as true r horrible ideas, your self-limiting beliefs will certainly deter you reaching your ultimate potential.

Thinking, "This will definitely never work" or, "I can't stand one more minute of the this," are going to derail you from your targets. It's required to comprehend when your mental state turns into being overly pessimistic.

Speak to your personal like you 'd talk with a buddy. When your thoughts come to be catastrophic or unhelpful, respond with a greater realistic statement that confirms your capability to deal with your struggles.

You can even create a concept that you duplicate throughout tough times.

Number 5.
Build Mental Stamina.

Building psychological power corresponds to building physical toughness. While you may not consider your mental muscle mass till you require it the absolute most, a problem isn't always the best time to construct intellectual stamina.

Similarly, you don't prefer to wait till you have to carry a heavy object to start building bodily strength, right? Pumping iron for 5 minutes before you go move a couch is not going to do you plenty good. But step by step building strength over time can make sure you have the muscle you want when you have extra weight to carry.

Think of mental strength in the same way. There will be times when you are going to need all the mental strength you can muster. So, it is essential to make intellectual exercise a day by day habit.

Chapter 2: Financial

Number 6
Take a hard look your family's finances.

Do you have an emergency fund? How massive is it? How many paychecks can you miss before you run out of money? How much budget flexibility do you have? How many bills need to be paid every month? Is your current financial scenario comfy or stressful? Don't beat yourself up if things are tight but realize that you can be in control of your cashflow and you have the strength to improve your situation. Sometimes, admitting previous mistakes is the first step to making changes.

Number 7
Add Income and Extra Cash

Most of us have some ways to create some extra cash fast, but sometimes it can be challenging to come up with things to do. Don't wait until the crisis hits before you start exploring ways to make extra cash! You cannot depend on your 9-5 or the government to put food on your table. I suggest that everyone should have multiple streams of income. In the time of a crisis, that other income source may determine whether you can feed your family or not.

Number 8
Pay Off Debt Before Crisis and Add Income

Large debt payments will strangle you in an economic emergency. Stop the using your credit cards, and don't take on any new loans. Make a plan to pay off your cards. If you have automobile payments, evaluate your options: can you certainly manage to pay for the payment, is the automobile suitable for your financial situation, and may you be better off with some other vehicle?

Another thing you should do is Add an income. Relying on a single income is difficult. Consider if your family can support another job, whether it is a 2nd job for the head of the household or a first or second job for a spouse. Maybe you can't do it forever, but you can do it for a few months to build up a savings account or pay off debt.
☐
Number 9
Trim your ongoing expenses.

Call your cable company and ask how you can lower your bill. Comparison shop your smartphone service. Consider methods to limit your gasoline spending, including planning trips, carpooling, strolling or biking when possible. Unplug your television, cable box, computer and cellphone chargers, and different electronics when not in use.

Try the "no spend" method. Have a "no spend" day, weekend or week to see how well you can "make do" with what you have. Appreciate everything you have.

Number 10
Start an emergency fund.

If you are actually living paycheck to paycheck and you lose your job throughout a financial crisis, you are at threat for losing your property as well as living in poverty. It's not always easy to find yet another job and also replace your revenue. Your objective needs to be actually to conserve up sufficient money to deal with 6 months of costs. These funds should go into your emergency fund.
•   If you are trying to get out of debt, save up an emergency fund of $1,000 and then apply all of your extra income to your debt. Once your debt is paid off, you can divert more money into your emergency fund.
•   Keep your emergency fund separate from your checking account so that you are not tempted to use the money. Put it in a low-risk, interest-bearing account such as a savings account, money market account or certificate of deposit (CD).

•   On the other hand, a complete economic collapse would leave you unable to access your bank account, because of the crash of the financial system. Additionally, your money may become useless or extremely devalued. Consider stocking other commodities that you could barter with in an economic collapse, like alcohol, precious metals (gold and silver), and fuel.☐

Chapter 3. Protection

The tips in this chapter are very important because it could literarily mean life or death. In a crisis, things can turn bad quickly and people will get desperate. Here are some things that you can do to protect yourself and your family.

Number 11
Protect Your Home

Identify safe rooms, meeting spots, and emergency supplies. Criminals report being actually discouraged through factors such as seeing an automobile in a driveway, a dog, hearing songs or even tv within, or even a security alarm going off. Make your house as unappealing of a target as possible.

Establish an alarm system at home. Wireless surveillance units are simple and affordable to install and also sustain. These alarms inform you if an intruder is approaching your home.

□
Number 12
Protect Your Family

Remember the earthquake and fire drills we did as children in school? Families can have comparable drills, just in case. What would you do, and where would you meet up if God forbid you found yourself in the middle of a home intrusion scenario? Talk it through in advance. Some parents are afraid to discuss preparation with their children, although others believe it is better than the alternative.

Number 13
Self Defense

I don't desire to recommend violence, however every adult and maybe even adolescents have to practice some type of self-defense. Whether it's martial arts or studying how to use a gun property. You're never know if you or one of your family members will need to use self-defense to break out of a bad situation. Google local self-defense instructors in your location and join a class. Also, if you determine to get a gun for your home, please first get a gun license, a safe for the weapon, then sign up for weapon safety class. If you prefer not to use a gun then here a few alternative self-defense tools:
•	Mace and pepper spray can be sprayed into an attacker's face to give you time to get away.

•	Hand-held stun guns deliver a large electrical shock to stun the attacker.
•	Taser devices shoot two small probes a distance of up to 15 feet that transmit an electrical charge to the attacker.
•	Sonic alarms create a loud noise to let others know that you are in trouble.

Number 14
Protect Your Health

Health Insurance may or may not be available to you and your family during a Government Shutdown or economic crisis, therefore maintaining your health is important to survival. Of course, some health conditions are unavoidable and a trip to the doctor is required, but many conditions can be treated with simple home remedies. Start familiarizing yourself with home remedies, because they will save you money! ☐

Number 15
Protect Your Resources

Carry identification, credit cards, devices, and chargers always. Duplicate essential documents such as your driver´s license and passport in case you or loved ones back need the information when the actual documents are not in your possession.

Make plans for your pets at home in case your return is delayed and remember that many shelters don't allow them. Lastly put all of your important documents along with spare car keys in a safe that way your family members can have easy access to them if needed. Also, if you have spare keys for a second home or grandparents, or friend of the family's house, put them inside the safe as well. If you need to go in a hurry, all of your important things will be in one place and you won't have to look for them!
☐

Chapter 4. Health

Healthcare Insurance can be affected during a government shutdown or crisis therefore it's important that you take the necessary steps to keep you and your family healthy during these times.

Number 16
Develop Healthy Lifestyle Habits

Your way of living options either relieve or even complement the threats you take when you go without health plan. If you would love to lessen those threats, after that be additional cautious along with your lifestyle selections. Drink alcoholic drinks exclusively in small amounts. Do not smoke. Don't make use of leisure medicines. Consume a wholesome diet regimen. Sustain a well-balanced body weight, acquire exercise, limit your sodium consumption, drink water instead of soda pops, clean your palms frequently, comb as well as floss your pearly whites twice a time.

Number 17
Budget for Emergencies

When you do without health insurance, you possess nothing but your very own sources to rely upon for your medical costs. You will need to plan and budget for emergencies.

Number 18
Home Remedies

Again, it's time to learn some home remedies that you can use to treat yourself if you become sick! A good resource to use is a book a book called "Home Remedies from Grandma" by Derrick Mitchell. This book has remedies for all kinds of issues, common cold, flu, migraines, muscle pains, etc.

Number 19
Keep First Aid Kits Handy

A first aid kit is an important thing to have around in case of an emergency. Your first aid kit should be easily accessible and portable. You aren't going to be able to pack the kitchen sink in it, but you want a first aid kit that's big enough to carry all of the basics.
□

Number 20
Public Health Departments

You can take advantage of public health clinics, private walk ins, or urgent care clinics. People with a severe cold, or flu symptoms, broken bones, or cuts that require stitches have several options:

•	County public health clinics, community health centers or free clinics provide care for free or on a sliding scale based on income.

•	Private walk-in or urgent care clinics. They generally require payment at the time of service, but many will list their prices at the front desk so at least you know what you're getting into.

Chapter 5: Food

Food shortages are inevitable in a government shutdown or economic crisis. As The food industry operates on very small earnings margins and can only live on when invoices are paid quickly. As severe inflation cripples marginal businesses, which include suppliers, wholesalers, and retailers, payments will cease. As inflation persists, extra groups will fail, and food will turn out to be a scarce commodity.

Number 21
Stockpile food

Start stockpiling early. Make ample area to keep freeze-dried meals, canned items, and dry goods and check that the temperature and humidity requirements on your preps match the climate of your storage space.

Keep a balanced stockpile of nutritious, mineral, and energy-rich foodstuffs. You'll need to make certain that your meals have enough protein, vitamins, fats, minerals, and carbohydrates to maintain your immune system and your energy. Salt is a wonder-ingredient for curing beef, retaining fish, and adding flavor to otherwise bland dishes. Plus, it by no means goes bad!

If you want a complete list of all foods that you should add to your stockpile check out my other book titled "Survival Foods" by Everett Moss. This book is also on amazon.

Number 22
Water Source

Water isn't meals however it is necessary for your stockpile. If you have three months' worth of food however only a week's worth of water, you won't survive unless you locate alternate water sources.

Number 23
Multiple ways to cook

How would you cook dinner your meals if your electrical energy wasn't available? What if you needed a way to keep decrease your monthly utility bill? Invest a wooden or charcoal grill, additionally a gas grill can come in accessible as well. Just make sure that you have a few back up propane tanks.
☐

Number 24
Grow your own food

Learn to Grow your Own Food. Start practicing your gardening skills now while you have time, so that you can master them and immediately begin growing your crops. Just imagine, your back yard could be your grocery store during a financial crisis.

Number 25
MRE (Meals Ready to Eat)

An MRE is a self-contained complete meal. One MRE equals one meal. The packaging of an MRE is designed to withstand rough conditions and exposure to the elements. These meals are used by militaries around the world as food rations. It's a good idea to have these meals in your stockpile because they are easy to prepare, and they supply a balanced meal.

Chapter 6: Community

People who are members of communities have more benefits and the communities can help them in tough times. Here is how a community will help you in your hard times.

Number 26
Learn what services your community has to offer.

Many neighborhood facilities and church buildings provide free offerings for people in need. Don't be ashamed to go to these places and ask for help or gather free food when its available. Every little bit helps!

Number 27
Become an Active Member

Get involved in your neighbors, nearby church, community center, fraternities, sororities, volunteer groups, clubs, etc.... Get to know the participants of your community and establish relationships. These people can grow to be your backbone throughout the tough times.

Number 28
GPS vs Map

We have come to be so accustom to the use of a GPS device to navigate to our destination, however what happens if your cell phone battery is low or if you lose service? Do you have a map of your area? Do you comprehend how to use a map? Do you have a compass? The following is a list of different types of maps.

City map: This map can help you figure out alternative street evacuation routes if bridges and/or overpasses are closed. Also, gridlock on major highways and freeways is a given, so you might need to plot a course around them.
Topographical map: A topo map is a three-dimensional view of an area. Looking at it, you can get an idea of the terrain.

State Highway map: This gives the big picture of your situation. It shows major highways and roads and gives general directions. It is useful for figuring out where to go once you escape the urban scene.

Forest Service map: I carry this in my car in central Oregon. Commonly referred to as a fire road map, this is a large overview of the national forests and public lands. Most importantly, it shows fire and logging roads. The map doesn't show if the roads are improved or not, so don't depend on this map to tell you if you can drive on it. In some instances, the roads may have overgrown into trails.

These maps are particularly useful for big game hunters. Kill an animal, and you need to know where the nearest road or trail is so you can get the meat out. It can also help you figure alternative routes in wilderness areas.

Number 29
Networking

Network with members from your community. Get to know people who you can learn different survival skills from. Join groups that teach financial freedom, gardening, outdoor activities etc.

Number 30
Facebook Groups and Communities

Facebook can be used more than simply to socialize and to look at your friends' photos. There are a ton of Facebook groups that offer all sorts of understanding and assistance to its members.

Chapter 7 Knowledge

Number 31
Read Books

Read this book, after that you're already on the ideal path. You'll end up being a survival sponge and also absorb as much knowledge as you can on this subject because your survival might depend on it eventually.
Blog Sites
There are some actually good Survival Blog site sites online. Do a google search and you will certainly find all kinds of survival websites in the search results.

Number 32
In addition to your regular job, make sure you have skills that you'd need in a traditional economy, such as farming, cooking, or repair.

Number 33
News Outlets

Although some individuals think that we are residing in the "fake information" era, you still need to pay attention to what's being reported in the news. Stay up to day with the present occasions to ensure that you can remain prepared.

Number 34
Identify Resources

If you remain in the army, recognize resources to help you if money gets tight. Your branch's emergency alleviation society is a great area to begin.
- Army Emergency Situation Alleviation
- Navy-Marine Corps Relief Society
- Flying Force Aid Society
- Shore Guard Mutual Help Society

If you are a noncombatant employee call your banks as well as bank card companies and supply an explanation for the scenario. A lot of them will be inclined to help you at some point of this time of shutdown. Talk to your banks or savings union to see if they are providing interest-free lending for missed out on incomes.

Ask if they have any type of certain programs for the federal government closure. Make certain to consist of lenders who are expecting settlement using an allotment. If you're not going to have the ability to make a payment promptly, tell them up front and also ask what the consequences will certainly be. Inquire to waive late costs or other added costs for late repayments.
☐

Number 35

Engage with your legislators and stay informed. While it is not a direct step to boosting capital, the most concrete activity you can take towards ending the closure is requiring time to contact your legislators as well as advise them to do something they can to boost the circumstance in D.C.

The real way we can make a difference is take that six minutes and send an electronic mail to your congressmen. Let them know this is now not what we meant when we voted for you guys. ☐

Chapter 8 Planning

We've briefly talked about planning in some of the other chapters but let's really dig a little bet deeper. Here are the top 5 things that you need to do to plan for a government shutdown or economic crisis.

Number 36
Increase your emergency fund

One of the excellent actions you can do to reduce a shutdown's impact is to assemble up a reserve. Consider having sufficient money handy to preserve your family members or business afloat for at the very least 3 months and maintain paying your expenses. If your reserve is currently low, consider altering protections in your portfolios, such as shares as well as mutual funds, into liquid properties. You should start saving extra of your contemporary income as well.

Number 37
Contact your bank

Do not wait till you're in the middle of a federal government closure prior to you contacting the bank services you rely upon. Let your bank understand right now just how a federal government shutdown may affect your capital; it may want to supply you a low-interest credit line to aid you. Likewise, let your bank card as well as home mortgage companies learn about your scenario as well. Some loan providers, most of whom depend greatly on business with government employees, may provide various loaning terms for you momentarily to decrease the strike of a shutdown.

Number 38
Review your budget

Now is a remarkable time to evaluate your family budget, and also assess whether you need to make some serious alterations as a government closure impend. Perhaps it's time to tighten up the belt a bit. Reducing additional expenses, such as cable as well as mobile phone solutions, can save you thousands of bucks each month as well as improve your money scenario throughout a government closure.

Decreasing charge cards while you have the possibility to do so might make good sense as well. Because closure risks are coming to be repeating events, it likewise may be a great time to change your spending plan permanently to better make through this regrettable fad.

Number 39
Begin expanding your streams of earnings.

If you count very closely on the Federal Government or Government Contracting for your revenue, then it may be prudent to begin diversifying. Establish an objective in this year to have a boost in your individual income. Begin a business, online business, side hustle, get a sideline, make investments with your money. Beginning structure numerous streams of earnings now! Do not wait up until it's too late. There are masses of resources online that can aid you find the correct circulation of earnings for you.
If a closure continues for an extensive duration, you may furthermore wish to think about some brief work alternatives, too. Working as a consultant, also for a brief duration, can additionally aid produce sufficient money drift to maintain your solvent till the shutdown ultimately finishes.

Number 40
Get ready for backups

If a federal government shutdown takes place, and Congress cannot broker a bargain to discontinue it, what's your plan for the lengthy shutdown? Ultimately, your cash reserve is going to run out. Having a longer-term plan can aid stave off the panic as your money decreases and bills pile up. Luckily, you do have a few options to think about to help aid you throughout this moment.

You may be able to tap into your retirement savings if you have no income coming in; many different retirement accounts, such as the Federal Government's Thrift Savings Plan, will allow you to access these funds in the event of a dire situation. Other accounts may allow the same, so check in with your retirement plan manager.

Chapter 9 Preparing your Family

Number 41
Family members Fulfilling

You've already made your new family budget plan, currently it's time to collect every one of the participants in your home for a conference to discuss the budget plan and also the new lifestyle that you as well as your family will require to live in order to survive theses tough times. Describe to your children that funds will be tight therefore you as a household will have to reduce on some points that you're accustom too as well, like maybe entertainment, eating out, new clothes, buying etc. Ideally this will certainly simply be momentary until things come back on the right track.

Number 42
Keep calm and carry on

A government shutdown is challenging, don't make it worse by panicking and also doing genuine damage to your family, company, or funds. Avoid making drastic temporary monetary steps, such as liquidating all your investments, or investing in something you recognize little concerning. Adhere to your strategy.

Do not do anything that seriously affects your company because of the hazard of a closure, either. Bear in mind, the Federal Government will certainly come back active right after the closure, so don't melt any type of bridges.

Number 43
Leave the country if needed

See to it your passport is up to date in case you 'd need to leave the country on short notice. Research study target countries now as well as take a trip there vacationing, so you recognize with your destination. If you have friends in other countries, reach out to them and connect.

Number 44
Fitness as well as Outdoors

Maintain yourself and your household. Get in top physical shape. Know basic survival abilities, such as self-defense, foraging, searching, and also learn how to start a fire. Exercise, go camping, learn the outdoors. journeys. If you can, relocate near a wildlife preserve in a warm climate. In this way, if a collapse takes place, you can live off the land in a fairly unpopulated area.
☐

Number 45
Improve your negative practices

Are you wasting money? Some of your daily behaviors can cost you. Come to be a frugal patriot! Find out just how to save cash for even more preparations.
Here are some good routines:
- Stop going to the films during the night. You can see the exact same motion picture as a matinee and save big bucks. Additionally, you can view flicks totally free with your Amazon.com Prime subscription or obtain a bargain on Netflix.
- Go all-natural. Grow your hair long or have longer intervals between haircuts, miss the manicure/ pedicure, do not obtain yet an additional tattoo or puncturing.
- Stand up to the urge and suppress your addiction. To put it simply, gave up cigarettes, consume alcohol just one beer or glass of wine, forgo taking the youngsters for gelato, avoid the baristas, quit getting the morning bagel, bring a lunch to function and conserve money on your day-to-day bad habits.
- Become a spendthrift. Check out yard sales and also second hand shops if you require something.
- Save money on gas. Are you getting the appropriate sort of gas? Are you idling? Before you take your cars and truck on a spin. If you have more than one automobile after that begin carpooling. A few basic suggestions as well as techniques can conserve you hundreds of dollars on gas.

Chapter 10 Additional Bonus Tips

Number 46
Transfer credit card financial debt to a 0% APR card

You can transfer your debt to one or more 0% APR cards. With a 0% APR charge card, you frequently can defer your existing balance as well as brand-new purchases for as much as 12-18 months. That indicates you won't owe any kind of repayments other than the minimal settlement until the 0% APR period finishes. Interest will additionally not build up during this moment. While this technique will certainly not make your debt disappear, it will assist postpone your financial debt and also interest costs. Make sure to repay your new card balance in full before the 0% APR duration ends.

Number 47
Negotiate with suppliers

If you have repeating subscriptions or other monthly costs, currently is an opportune time to bargain with company for a possible decrease of your costs, or a minimum of a deferment of your charges. That includes your lease or mortgage, exclusive student loans, auto repayments, fitness center membership and comparable costs. Significantly, if there are no termination fees or if you get on a month-to-month subscription strategy, take into consideration cancelling (temporarily or completely) non-essential services.

Number 48
Switch to an income-driven payment

If you have student loans now is a good time to consider an income-driven payment plan. With an income-driven repayment strategy, your monthly strategy hinges on your revenue, household dimension, state of residency as well as various other elements. If you are affected by the federal government shutdown, you could qualify for a reduced month-to-month payment plan, which might be as low as $0. With income-driven repayment plans, you can change strategies at a later date.

Number 49
Re-finance your loans

Without an income, it can be testing to pay your loans. For several, despite an income, it's not always simple either. Provided the current climbing rates of interest rates, it's a positive time to refinance loans. Student and car loan refinancing, enables you to receive a new funding with a reduced rate of interest, a solitary regular monthly payment. The reduced rate of interest conserves you money on interest every month and assist you pay off loan faster.

Number 50
Food Safety

Should you be stressed over the security of your food during the federal government closure? The answer is complex, as well as it depends who you ask. You should be concerned that the shutdown might cause gaps in food safety and security. What foods should you keep away from during a closure? I would say anything you aren't regulating on your own, so any type of fresh, uncooked items on the marketplace location, such as ready-to-eat salads and also prepackaged sandwiches, or dishes that aren't cooked.

Checklist: Sprouts, leafed greens, ready to consume products like cheese, gelato. I would certainly be specifically suspect if you're an expecting lady, child, or people with a compromised body immune system. I would certainly keep away from it entirely.

My suggestions is for people to proceed utilizing good sense steps. Rinse off their vegetables, rinse off you fruits, cook your meat, do not consume raw meats, and just do all the regular things that you ought to do all the time anyhow and you'll be ok when it pertains to food security.

☐

Conclusion

Thank again for taking out time to read this book! I hope that it will give you some tools to help you prepare for the next government shutdown or economic crisis. If you apply the concepts in this book to your life you will be much more prepared for what's to come. In addition to this book I have a series of books coming out called the "Survivor Series". You can get the next book in this series for free by going to the link below.

https://dl.bookfunnel.com/paaumw1bcj

Resources

https://federalnewsnetwork.com/mike-causey-federal-report/2019/01/shutdown-survival-guide-the-8-day-rule/

https://www.survivalsullivan.com

https://www.katehorrell.com/government-shutdown-to-do/